www.providencebooks.net

Publisher Contact

Email:contact@providencebooks.net

Social media: facebook.com/providencebooks

Acknowledgements

The team at Providence Books would like to thank our friends, family, suppliers and customers for making our vision of creating the highest-quality books a reality. Thanks for purchasing and enjoy the quotes!

This page is intentionally left blank

This page is intentionally left blank

'Get a Job' is about all the rich kids we knew when we were younger, kids who never had jobs but always had money for partying or getting their hair done.

Beth Ditto

A beautiful plant is like having a friend around the house.

Beth Ditto

A few years back, when my style was 'punk grandma,' I picked up an amazing pair of sandals - orthopaedic ones, with really thick soles. I've given them away to a friend now, because these days my look is more '1980s substitute teacher gone wild.'

Beth Ditto

A weird thing about Gossip that I've always said: 'If I weren't in this band, I would never listen to it.' But I would go see it. It's a band you would go see that you don't necessarily listen to. We've always wanted to do a live album because personally, I think we're a way better band live than on record.

Beth Ditto

ABBA was a direct influence on me.

Beth Ditto

All this fashion stuff - who's cool now - is just a bigger version of the cool kids versus the nerds.

Beth Ditto

Aretha Franklin was a teenage mom, a musician who came from an incredibly Christian background, but there was a lot of love, which is really inspiring in a feminist way.

Beth Ditto

As a kid, I was always mad - just noticing the women at Thanksgiving, running around the kitchen, while the men were watching football. For one, I don't want to cook, and for two, I hate football. I was stuck in the middle.

Beth Ditto

As with most phobias, the fear of flying does make some sense, but if ever there was a fear worth quashing then this is it. After all, life is short, and there's a great big world to explore out there.

Beth Ditto

Because I didn't have any queer, lesbian, female role models I hated my own femininity and had to look deep within myself to create an identity that worked for me. Pop culture just doesn't hand us enough variety to choose from.

Beth Ditto

Do I ever think Gossip will be really massive in America? No, I don't think it'll happen - and that's fine. It's kind of nice because I get to experience everything at once. I get to come home and it not be weird, like in Paris or something. It is nice to be completely anonymous.

Beth Ditto

Even if you're only wearing trainers and a vest, eyeliner will instantly transform you. People always look put-together when their make-up's on and their eyes are popping - just ask Amy Winehouse!

Beth Ditto

Even talking, I'm super-loud. I could never have that kind of meek, little wispy whimsical lavender and lace voice. It comes from my body. There's no way I can fight it.

Beth Ditto

For me the greatest revenge of all is having a happy adulthood, waking up in my gorgeous turquoise bedroom in the morning beside a person who really inspires me. That's the best revenge a girl-loving girl from the Bible belt could possibly have. And, importantly, it's healthy.

Beth Ditto

For my group of friends is Lady Gaga eye-opening? No. She's a less dangerous version of what was so cool about pop culture in the '80s. Back then it was so gay and so punk in so many ways.

Beth Ditto

For years now I have run a kitchen-sink punk salon in my house, called Salon du Gay. In the early days, people would pay for a riot grrrl bob or a passable bleach job with a mixtape, $3 or a selection of baked goods - whichever they could afford. More recently though, with Gossip doing well, I've performed these punk hair transformations for free.

Beth Ditto

Girls are taught to sing high and pretty, like Antony, not low and from the guts like Nina Simone. But we're slowly trying to change that. There are so many things we're not told growing up, and it's our true feminist responsibility to take the truth to the people who need to hear it.

Beth Ditto

Granny Ditto always referred to perfume as 'smell good' and for me it's an essential. I have a sweetheart who's extremely allergic to most scents, so I have to be extra careful - as well as creative - in the smell department. The key, I've found, are essential oils, which come in all kinds of 100% natural scents.

Beth Ditto

Growing up as a chubby kid with a ton of imaginary friends and a Cyndi Lauper obsession, I learned about rejection early on and was constantly trying to avoid it.

Beth Ditto

Here is my prescription to heal all wounds. Watch the film 'Funny Girl' at least five times, eat at least 45 chocolate bars, and hang out with all those friends you blew off to hang out with your ex. I truly believe that, through a combination of Nutella, old pals and Barbra Streisand, we can achieve happiness and, very probably, world peace.

Beth Ditto

High school wasn't so bad though because, by then, I had worked out that there were far more nerdy kids and poor kids than there were rich, popular kids, so, at the very least, we had them outnumbered.

Beth Ditto

I always was really confident about myself, about my voice, myself as a person, my body, all of those things, but as a songwriter - I just didn't identify as a songwriter at all.

Beth Ditto

I believe I owe all the best parts of my adulthood to embracing my imperfections and showcasing them.

Beth Ditto

I can take care of a house, and some people I meet, I think, 'You don't even know how to make a bed.'

Beth Ditto

I certainly know first hand the waste one lady can create through her primping routine, because I am a victim of fashion: to me a day without makeup and a bouffant to match is a day wasted. I love it all - whether it's fancy, cheap or, I'm ashamed to say, even if it's bad for the environment.

Beth Ditto

I don't feel famous and I didn't want my autobiography to be like a Paris Hilton story.

Beth Ditto

I don't have a good attention span and can't spend long in record stores or video shops or games emporiums without getting grumpy.

Beth Ditto

I feel sorry... for people who've had skinny privilege and then have it taken away from them. I have had a lifetime to adjust to seeing how people treat women who aren't their idea of beautiful and therefore aren't their idea of useful, and I had to find ways to become useful to myself.

Beth Ditto

I have a lot of feminist idols. My favorite thing about growing up in Arkansas - well, not favorite but something I've always felt grateful for - was that I really had to dig for what I could. There was no Internet. There wasn't tons of feminist literature floating around.

Beth Ditto

I have been 130 lbs. as well as 215 lbs. I have had blond, strawberry blond, green, pink and purple hair, and none of that has ever exempted me from having lewd comments flung at me in the street.

Beth Ditto

I have no control over what people think of me but I have 100% control of what I think of myself, and that is so important. And not just about your body, but so many ways of confidence. You're constantly learning how to be confident, aren't you?

Beth Ditto

I just like food too much, and I don't want to change. I spent so much of childhood trying to change, and I just got sick of it... I don't want to look like Britney Spears, I just don't want to. She's hideous.

Beth Ditto

I knew that if I wanted to stop being a pushover I had to get comfortable with small rejections myself. That took some work, but because of it I can now say 'no' to other people with a clear conscience.

Beth Ditto

I love Adele so much and it's honestly not because we're both big.

Beth Ditto

I love sad songs. They say so much. I love country music but even the happy songs sound really sad.

Beth Ditto

I mean, if I was living to please people, I'd have never been in a band at all. I wouldn't have anything awesome around. I'd just be bored.

Beth Ditto

I really worshipped Mama Cass a lot. Mama Cass, who was really fat and she didn't lose weight. Yeah, she went on diets but for the most part of her life and the better part of her career she was a big person.

Beth Ditto

I shave my body in all kinds of ways, wear tons of eyeliner and dye my hair pink.

Beth Ditto

I think it's really cool that there are people like Adele on the cover of 'Vogue' and 'Rolling Stone,' and like I think it's really important that people are talking about your body, because if they don't, then you'll never be able to break that barrier.

Beth Ditto

I think that for the five-year-old watching MTV right now, Lady Gaga is going to be an iconic person. In 20 years, the people who are here and talking to journalists will be like, 'Oh Lady Gaga changed my life, Nicki Minaj changed my life.' They'll be saying who influenced them and it will be Lady Gaga, Nicki Minaj, artists like that.

Beth Ditto

I thought to be feminine was to give in to straight culture, or the beauty standard, but in my heart I had a flair for fashion and style. They were passions I kept secret because I didn't understand I could love clothes and hair and makeup and still like girls.

Beth Ditto

I want to make the IKEA of clothes for fat girls and boys. Cheap, affordable, basic - but ethically made. Basics, you know? Like Spanx - I'm still confused as to why retailers haven't ripped them off yet and done it well. It's because they don't understand the basics behind it. I love Spanx. I'm wearing 'em right now!

Beth Ditto

I was always being told off at school. The teachers would say: 'Everyone's talking, but you're the one I can hear.'

Beth Ditto

I was born fat and have always been, which was just fine and even healthy and cute until I turned ten or so. Puberty hit like a hurricane and brought a new set of rules. All of a sudden it was my fault I was chubby.

Beth Ditto

I was born to be married. I just feel comfortable there. I love the idea of being partnered for ever. I love my girlfriend, we've been best friends since I was 18. There's not a thing we haven't been through except for marriage... We've had talks about what we would name our kids since we were in our 20s.

Beth Ditto

I was brought up by a single mom in a poor town in Arkansas and while some aspects of small-town life were really positive - like the fact that everyone there is really sweet and hospitable - there is also this close-minded mentality, and that naturally made me want to rebel.

Beth Ditto

I was given baby doll toys myself, and they proved a stark reminder that my life was expected to revolve around childbearing - just as my mom's had before me, and her mom's had before her.

Beth Ditto

I was overcome by the Holy Ghost one time, but in a Baptist way. I was six or seven, and I was saved. I just cried and cried. It was joy!

Beth Ditto

I work really well under pressure but I really hate doing things on a timeframe.

Beth Ditto

I worshipped Ethel Merman and I worshipped Ethel Merman a lot. It's incredible - Ethel Merman was a conventional singer. Her naming her child Ethel Merman, Jr., was, to me, one of the coolest feminist things.

Beth Ditto

I'm 90% performer, 10% musician. I've always said that Gossip are a band I would go see, not a band I would listen to.

Beth Ditto

I'm a feminist, of course, and I feel as if I'm very politically correct, although I do question what's P.C. and what's not - I don't just accept what I'm told.

Beth Ditto

I'm a great believer in karma, and the vengeance that it serves up to those who are deliberately mean is generally enough for me.

Beth Ditto

I'm constantly thinking about what I'll do next. I never count on music being a career of longevity. I mean, longevity is key, and I hope that it lasts, but you just don't know, because it's not in your hands, you don't make the decision.

Beth Ditto

I'm naturally a mousy blonde, so I dye my hair, and my eyebrows would disappear if I didn't get through at least a pencil a month.

Beth Ditto

I'm not sure that I am able to feel embarrassment.

Beth Ditto

I'm passionate about color. My best friend and I sit and look at Pantone books for fun.

Beth Ditto

I'm shameless, and I love a pun. There's a lot of Beth puns.

Beth Ditto

I've belched a lot more since I had gall bladder surgery. I don't know why.

Beth Ditto

I've had a ton of fast-food jobs - it changes your approach to human interaction forever.

Beth Ditto

I've had people ask me in interviews what it's like to have money, but that's not how it is. I have a middle-class life. I have a room in London but not a house, nor a BMW.

Beth Ditto

I've never had a very quiet voice. I tried in choir to make it smaller, and it just didn't work out. And I listened to a lot of soul music when I was growing up on my own accord. But I was mostly into Mama Cass and Gladys Knight, and they all had big voices too; just different than mine.

Beth Ditto

If you have a therapist who agrees with your every word, then your brain isn't getting proper exercise.

Beth Ditto

In moments when I question if I should be having kids, I think of all those phone calls from my sister-in-law, in which, 3,000 miles away, I hear my nephews screaming for her attention. I tell her I have to go because I am packing to leave for Europe, and her tone flatlines: 'That must be nice.'

Beth Ditto

It's really hard for me to sometimes put myself out there, like 'Hey, how do you feel about making music together?' because maybe I'm afraid of rejection or I don't want to put anybody out. It's the Southerner in me, like, 'I don't mean to bother you but do you mind making a song?'

Beth Ditto

Just like my straight friends, I am repeatedly asked when I plan to have kids, and have been told many times, by various branches of my bloodline, that 'even lesbians can have babies these days.'

Beth Ditto

My dad liked to boil a squirrel head and suck the brains out the nose. Smaller than a chicken, bigger than a rat.

Beth Ditto

My life hasn't been conventional and it hasn't been linear. I've had to make it up as I've gone along, which has taught me a lot. If you don't accept the obvious options that are laid out for you, it's up to you to work out where you're going and to create your own specific rules and goals.

Beth Ditto

My mother told me Homer Ditto was not my father. Nope. Mom had had a fling with some other guy who was my dad. Some dude who didn't stick around too long who Mom was happy to get rid of. She chose Homer, and Homer chose me, so he lent me his name even though I didn't have his blood.

Beth Ditto

My number-one theory in life is that style is proportional to your lack of resources - the less you have, the more stylish you're likely to be.

Beth Ditto

My size has helped make me an amazing performer too. The cliche of the Funny Fat Friend: I absolutely was that character - I am that character... It's a complicated bag of tools I acquired, and I've put them all to work onstage.

Beth Ditto

Olympia was a town crawling with music. I was new to the whole punk scene. The culture shock continued; Olympia had bagels! We didn't have bagels in Arkansas. You could order vegetarian food all over town! It was so crazy to me - a place with so many vegetarians, the restaurants made special dishes for them?

Beth Ditto

Portland is a place where you can find a community as a feminist, a vegan or a fat activist. Artists, musicians, knitters, and filmmakers can all meet like-minded souls. It's proved the perfect place for me and all my punk friends.

Beth Ditto

Products are a must - full stop. I'm sorry to say it, but that bob won't look so sleek on its own - you need a little help. It doesn't have to be the high-end stuff that they sell in the salon. Products you find in the supermarket are just as good, and sometimes better.

Beth Ditto

Reclaiming the word 'fat' was the most empowering step in my progress. I stopped using it for insult or degradation and instead replaced it with truth, because the truth is that I am fat, and that's ok. So now when someone calls me fat, I agree, whereas before I would get embarrassed and emotional.

Beth Ditto

Some makeup companies have really good recycling policies, and it's worth finding out whether your favourites are among them. With MAC, for instance, you can take any of your old makeup containers into its shops, and the sweetest deal is that, once you've racked up six containers, you get a free lipstick or lip gloss.

Beth Ditto

Starting out really punk came from not knowing any better and listening to music like that, not knowing how to play music - well, still not knowing how to play music.

Beth Ditto

Thanks to capitalism, the importance placed on beauty has never been so manipulated. We are the guinea pigs force-fed ads that tell us how pathetic we are: that we will never be loved, happy or valuable unless we have the body, the face, the hair, even the personality that will apparently be ours, if only we buy their products.

Beth Ditto

There is no rule in the pink-triangle guide to coming out that you must wear a rainbow flag cap and organise a full band parade.

Beth Ditto

There is no shame like poor shame. It can make you warm and charming, bitter and resentful, all at once.

Beth Ditto

There is something to be said for people who have to work hard, be creative, produce what they have with little - or no - means. Those of us from poor homes have the advantage of thinking for ourselves and of knowing that when times get hard, things could always be worse.

Beth Ditto

This archaic idea - that a woman who is unmarried and childless at 30 is somehow unnatural - will probably always exist, and, like most social standards, it is ridiculous.

Beth Ditto

We all seek approval, and our mother's seal is usually the most important. The nitty gritty is that we have to accept ourselves, even if it is just to be ready for the next cut-down. Mom's blessing or not.

Beth Ditto

When I am made fun of in the press I just remember those days when I'd come home to find that the water had been turned off because my mother couldn't afford the bill. Suddenly, everything feels easier.

Beth Ditto

When I moved out of my mom's house at 18 I was almost as sad to leave her sewing machine behind as anything else.

Beth Ditto

When I was a kid, Ellen DeGeneres and Rosie O'Donnell were mere blips on the gaydar; and they were both still in the closet.

Beth Ditto

When I was a teenager I would lock myself in the bathroom for hours, bouffanting my hair like Patty Duke and trying to recreate Barbra Streisand's flawless eyeliner, only to comb it all out and wash it all off before stepping out into the world a butchish bisexual teen.

Beth Ditto

When you see a fantastic colour or cut in a magazine, perched up on some famous so-and-so's head, it's tempting to ask your stylist for the same, but do not be fooled. The hair in those fancy photos can be very high maintenance.

Beth Ditto

Why wear pants when you can wear a muumuu?

Beth Ditto

With a stretch belt, anything can be a dress - a dinner napkin, a tablecloth, even a towel. Just wrap and snap, and away you go in an incredible outfit. Another plus is that the belt will pull all eyes to your lovely curves, and they even look good around a coat or a jacket.

Beth Ditto

You know how people love to glamorize poverty? There's nothing glamorous about it. But it did make me really creative. Those days, I was literally taking t-shirts in the day and sewing them back together to make dresses for the night.

Beth Ditto

You know, either I'm too fat or I'm flavour of the month. I don't feel either, but maybe I'm both, who knows?

Beth Ditto

You live in this shadow that you're going to burn in Hell until you're saved. And I still worry about it a little. I don't believe in Heaven, but I do still fear Hell.

Beth Ditto

This page is intentionally left blank

This page is intentionally left blank

This page is intentionally left blank

This page is intentionally left blank

This page is intentionally left blank

www.ingramcontent.com/pod-product-compliance
Lightning Source LLC
Chambersburg PA
CBHW061943280526
45787CB00004B/1700